MUSIC THROUGH TIME

Pauline Hall & Paul Harris

Piano Book 3

CONTENTS

Music Department
OXFORD UNIVERSITY PRESS
Oxford and New York

1598
Tower Hill

Giles Farnaby
(1563–1640)

Boris Godunov, later the subject of an opera by Mussorgsky, became Tsar in Russia after seizing power. The following year the Globe Theatre, famous for its links with Shakespeare, was built south of the River Thames in London. Since large parts of the theatre were in the open air, it was only used during the summer months.

Farnaby was an important English composer of this period. He often gave his keyboard pieces descriptive titles such as A *Toye*, and *His Dreame*.

© Oxford University Press 1993

Printed in Great Britain
OXFORD UNIVERSITY PRESS, MUSIC DEPARTMENT, GREAT CLARENDON STREET, OXFORD OX2 6DP
Photocopying this copyright material is ILLEGAL.

In England, plans were being made for the first daily newspaper, to be called The Courant. In his modernization of Russia, Tsar Peter the Great insisted that his subjects wore European dress.

Daniel Purcell was the brother of the great composer Henry Purcell. Both men came from a family of English musicians who flourished as singers, organists, and composers in the 17th and 18th centuries.

Daniel Purcell
(*c*.1660–1717)

1714
Rigaudon

William Babell
(*c.*1690–1723)

Queen Anne died, having been the first monarch to rule
Great Britain after the Union of England and Scotland.
She had 17 children, all of whom died before they grew
up, and when she was crowned she was so fat that she
had to be carried to the throne.

William Babell was an English organist, harpsichordist,
violinist, and composer. A busy man!

4

Handel composed his oratorio *Judas Maccabeus*. It contains the famous tune 'See the Conquering Hero Comes.'

Wilhelm Friedemann was the eldest of J. S. Bach's sons, and a talented composer in his own right. 'Allemande' was the name given to a short, dance-like movement, originally a peasant dance.

1746
Allemande

Wilhelm Friedemann Bach
(1710–84)

1758
Trumpet Voluntary

John Bennett
(1725–84)

The telescope was invented by John Dollond. Britain's first canal, the Bridgewater canal, was built in Lancashire. Although it had no locks, it did boast a forty-foot-high aqueduct across the River Irwell.

John Bennett was an English organist and composer. He published relatively little music, but Handel is known to have bought some of it, and thought highly of him.

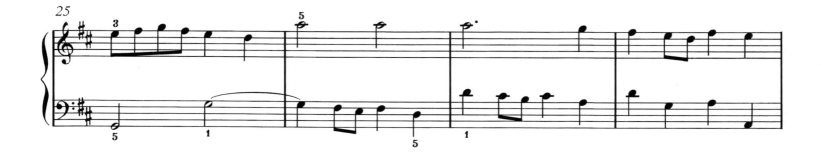

Myrtillia

Thomas Arne
(1710–78)

The explorer Captain James Cook and his crew became the first men to sail close to the South Pole. Four scientists independently discovered nitrogen gas, or 'noxious air' as they called it.

Thomas Arne was one of the most important English composers of his day. He wrote over 80 stage works, among them the masque *Alfred* which includes 'Rule Britannia', now always sung at the Last Night of the Proms.

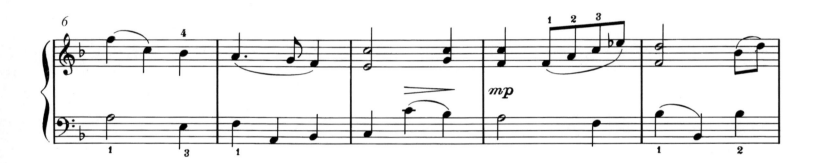

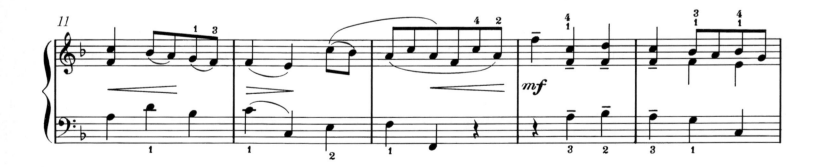

The British finally lost the American War of
Independence, after the battle of Yorktown. The planet
Uranus was discovered by the English astronomer
Herschel.

Mozart was perhaps the most talented child prodigy ever.
He was actually christened Johannes Chrysostomus
Wolfgangus Theophilus—quite a mouthful!

Les Echos

Wolfgang Amadeus Mozart

(1756–91)

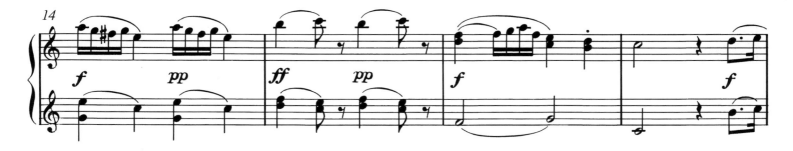

1787
Presto

Samuel Wesley
(1766–1837)

Dollar currency was introduced into the USA. In England, the Marylebone Cricket Club (known all over the world as the MCC) was formed, later establishing its headquarters at Lord's Cricket Ground.

Samuel Wesley was the second son of the Methodist Charles Wesley (who wrote the words to 'Hark! the herald angels sing'). He was regarded as the greatest organist of his day, and published a harpsichord tutor at the age of just eleven!

In Scotland, Robbie Burns wrote *Auld Lang Syne*—the song that is associated with New Year's Eve. Meanwhile, in France the Reign of Terror began. After the execution of Louis XVI and Marie Antoinette, even packs of playing cards were forbidden from having kings and queens.

Many of Haydn's symphonies have been given nicknames. This piece is from the second movement of his 'Clock' symphony (No. 101), so-called because of the 'tick-tock' accompaniment figure.

1794

Andante

Franz Joseph Haydn
(1732–1809)

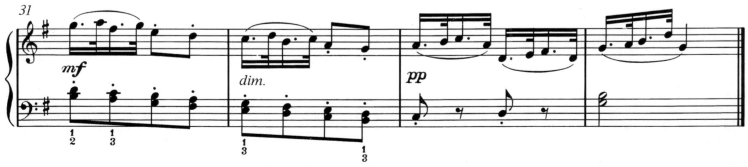

Napoleon Bonaparte was voted Consul for life by over three million Frenchmen. Also in this year, Beethoven composed his famous *Moonlight Sonata* for piano.

Boccherini was a prolific Italian composer who became famous as a virtuoso cellist while still a teenager. He lived in Spain for a while before becoming a composer at the Prussian court.

Minuet

Luigi Boccherini
(1743–1805)

1802
Menuetto

Ludwig Van Beethoven
(1770–1827)

While writing his second symphony this year, Beethoven noticed he was becoming deaf. His hearing got worse until he became totally deaf some seventeen years later. John Dalton introduced his atomic theory, the foundation of modern chemistry.

Beethoven wrote music in a great variety of musical forms, including symphonies, string quartets, and even a piece for four trombones. This minuet comes from one of his thirty-two piano sonatas.

Tempo di menuetto

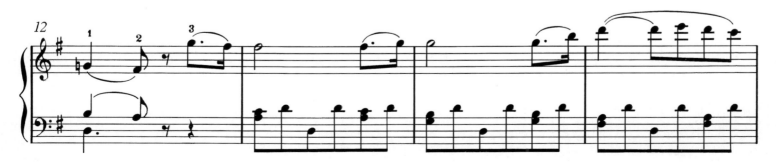

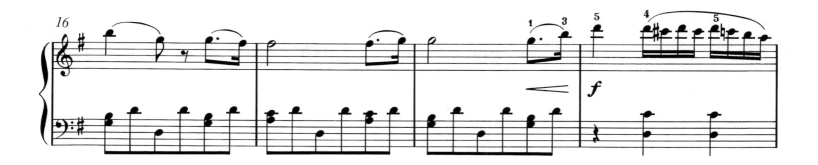

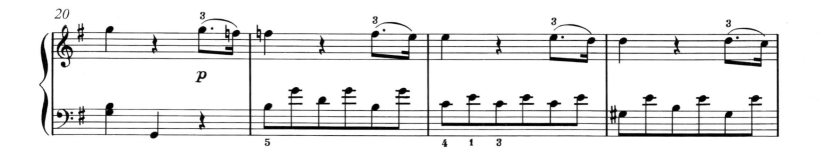

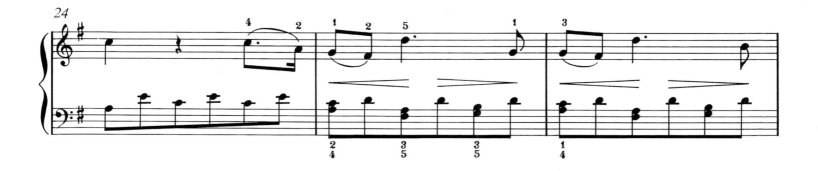

1851
Legend

Karl Czerny
(1791–1857)

The Great Exhibition opened in the 'Crystal Palace', including 13,000 exhibits from around the world. The sewing machine was invented, and London saw its first horse-drawn double-decker bus.

Czerny was an Austrian pianist and composer. He was a good friend of Beethoven, and an important teacher: his pupils included Franz Liszt, who was to become a great composer in his own right.

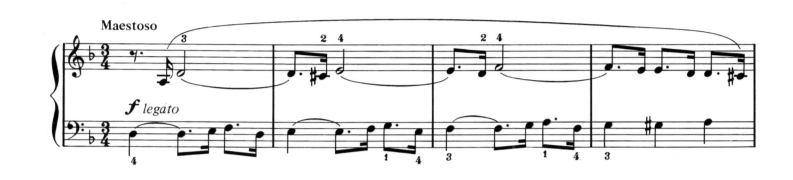

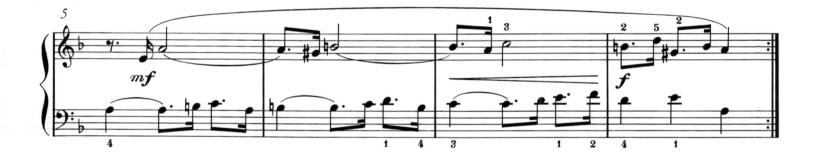

Abraham Lincoln, President of the USA, was assassinated in a Washington theatre by John Wilkes Booth, a failed actor.

German-born Johann Friedrich Burgmüller settled in Paris, establishing himself as a fashionable composer of songs, descriptive piano pieces for children, and stage works.

1865
Allegretto

Johann Friedrich Burgmüller
(1806–74)

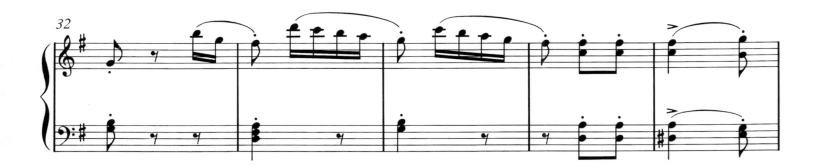

The buried ruins of the lost ancient city of Troy were
discovered on the west coast of Turkey. Excavations
revealed that Troy dates from at least 2000 BC.

Delibes began his musical career as a church organist, but
he was drawn to the theatre. He is best known for his ballets
Coppélia and *Sylvia*, both admired by no less a figure than
Tchaikovsky.

1870

Clockwork Toys

Léo Delibes
(1836–91)

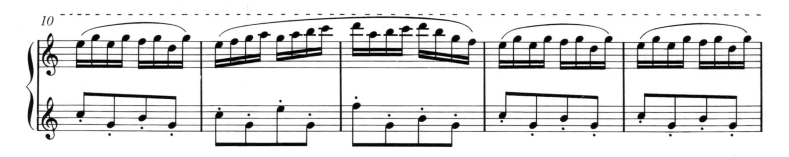

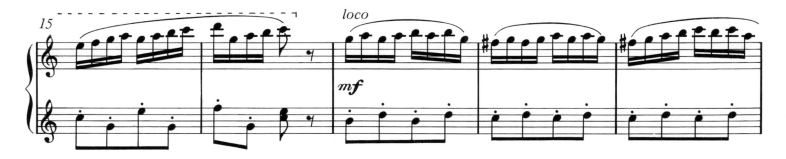

1874
Impromptu

The game of tennis was introduced to the USA, and in Philadelphia the first zoo opened. Monet's painting *Impression— Sunrise* gave its name to the term 'Impressionist'. The first exhibition of Impressionist paintings was held in Paris.

Impromptu literally means 'improvised' or 'on the spur of the moment'. Many 19th-century composers used the term for short instrumental pieces.

Cornelius Gurlitt
(1820–1901)

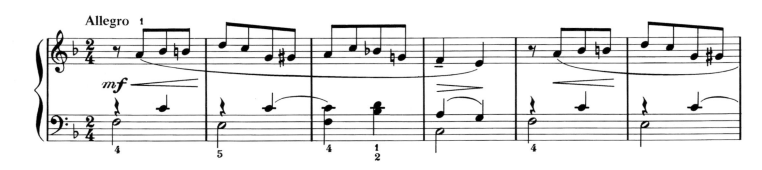

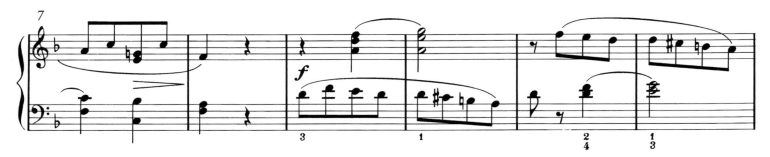

The first Woolworth's store opened in America, based on the new idea that all the goods were at two prices only: either five or ten cents. The first European telephone exchange opened in Paris, and Thomas Edison invented the light bulb.

Genari Karganov was a Russian composer who died at the early age of 32. He wrote many short character-pieces like this one.

1879
Little Waltz

Genari Karganov
(1858–1890)

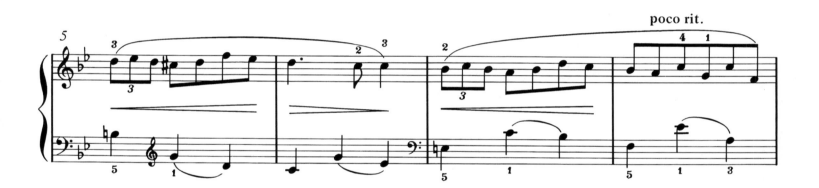

cont. over page

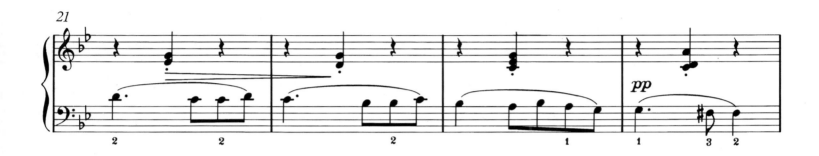

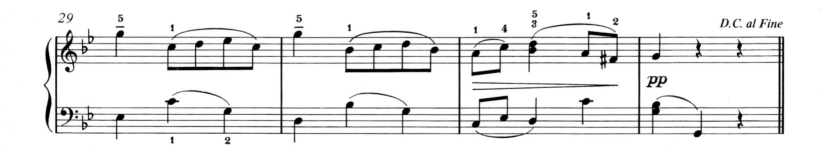

Mark Twain wrote *Huckleberry Finn*, the sequel to *Tom Sawyer*. It's about the adventures of a young boy in America at the time of the Mississippi steam boats.

Grieg is best known for his exciting Piano Concerto and the Peer Gynt suites. He was a Norwegian composer who often used his country's folk music to influence his melodies.

1884
My Homeland

Edvard Grieg
(1843–1907)

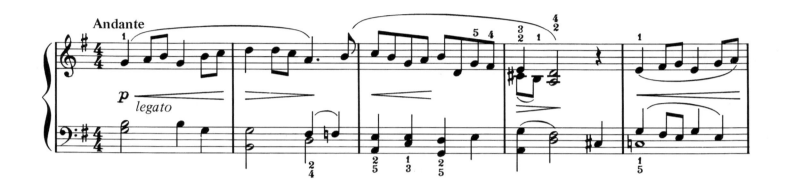

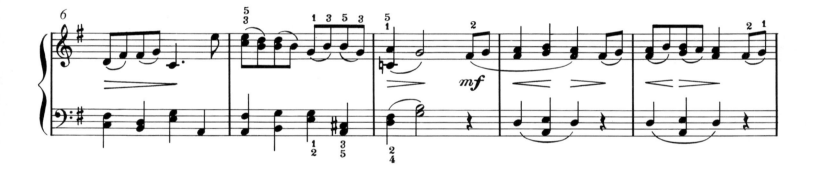

1893
Largo

Antonin Dvořák
(1841–1904)

Karl Benz in Germany and Henry Ford in the USA built their first motor cars. Alexander Graham Bell made the first long-distance telephone call, from Chicago to New York.

This is perhaps Dvořák's most famous melody. It comes from the slow movement of his Symphony No. 9, written during a three-year trip to the USA and known as the 'New World' Symphony. The tune is played by the cor anglais, a member of the oboe family.

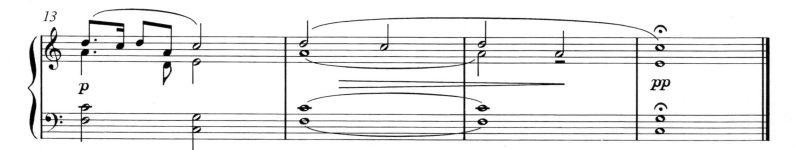

The world's largest refracting telescope was built at the Yerkes Observatory in Wisconsin, USA. It measures 102 centimetres in diameter.

Alexander Goedicke taught at the Moscow Conservatory in Russia. One of his most performed works is a concert study for trumpet, and he also wrote symphonies and concertos.

1897
Sonatina

Alexander Goedicke
(1877–1957)

1908
Cheese Cake Walk

Art Draper
(1884–1922)

The Wright brothers patented their 'flying machine'. Kenneth Grahame wrote one of the most popular children's books—*The Wind in the Willows*—the story of Mole, Ratty, Badger, and Toad.

The American jazz composer Art Draper lived in New Orleans—the home of jazz. He reportedly spent much of his time in a cake shop called Mills, and it may be that the title of this piece was inspired by his sweet tooth!

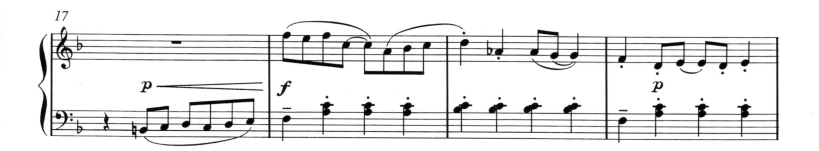

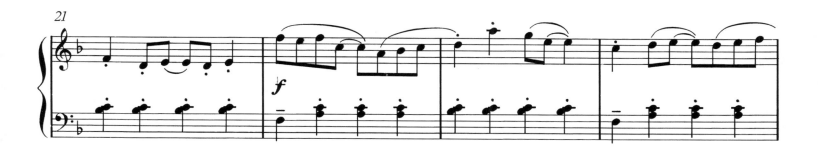

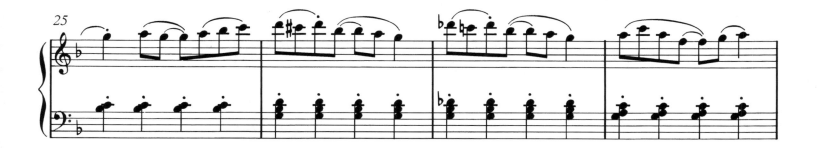

1913
Come Along Sam

Annie Curwen
(1845–1932)

The first crossword puzzle appeared in the *New York World*. In the last year of peace before World War I, Stravinsky's ballet *The Rite of Spring* caused a riot at its Paris première, and Charlie Chaplin made his first film.

In 1886 Annie Curwen, composer of this piece, wrote a famous piano tutor, *Mrs Curwen's Pianoforte Method*. It is still used by some teachers today.

Allegro moderato

1923
On Horseback

Alexander Grechaninov
(1864–1956)

Runaway inflation in Germany meant that £1 was worth about six million German marks. It took so many banknotes to buy even basic foods that many people used wheelbarrows to carry their money about! Wembley Stadium was used for the first time for the F. A. Cup Final—won by Bolton Wanderers.

Grechaninov studied with the great composer Rimsky-Korsakov. Born in Russia, he emigrated to Paris and then to the USA where he became an American citizen in 1946.

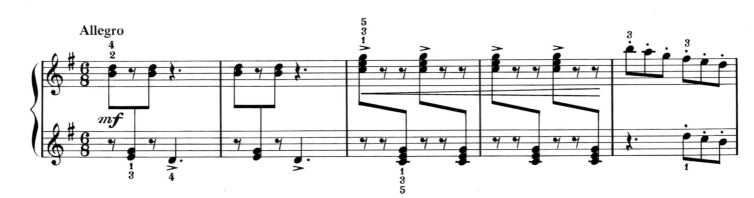

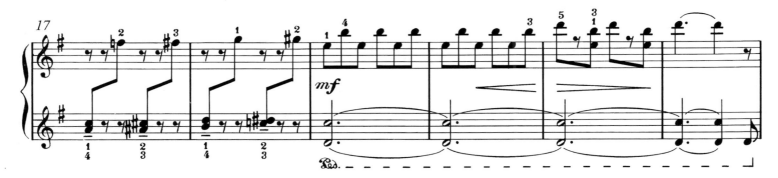

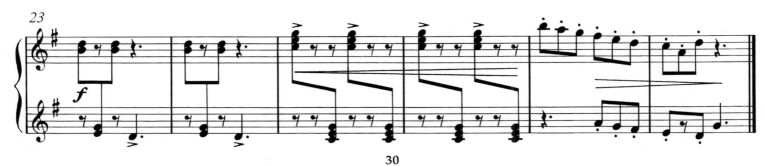

The film *King Kong* was made, and Sir Thomas Beecham founded the London Philharmonic Orchestra. In a year's time, Hindenburg, President of Germany, will appoint a new head of government—Adolf Hitler.

Sir Edward Elgar was one of the greatest English composers. Among his most famous pieces are the 'Pomp and Circumstance' Marches, which include the famous tune for 'Land of Hope and Glory', always sung at the Last Night of the Proms.

Edward Elgar
(1857–1934)

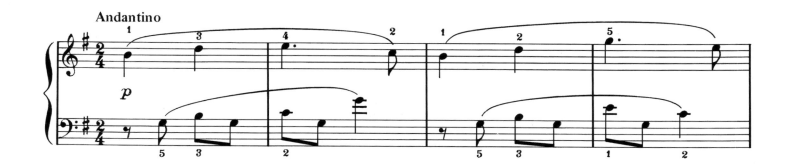

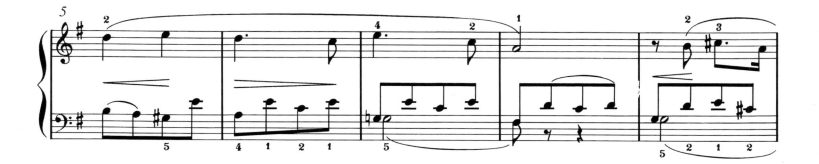

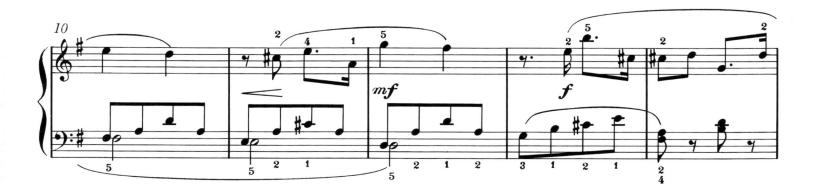

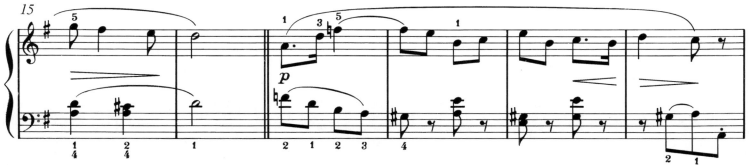

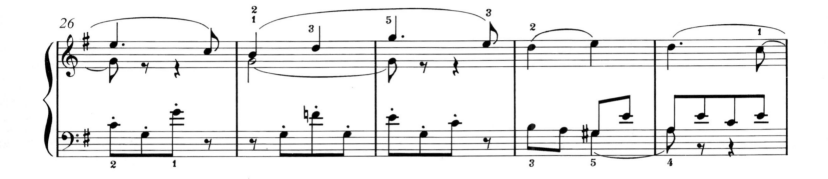

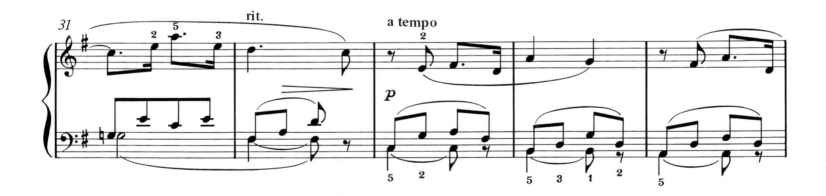

The mid-fifties saw the beginnings of a new style of popular music called Rock and Roll: artists like Chuck Berry, Elvis Presley, and Bill Haley and the Comets rose to stardom. Atomic power was first used in the USA, and the film *The Dambusters* was made.

C. S. Lang was born in New Zealand. As a school teacher he was very interested in educational music, writing many works for piano and organ.

C. S. Lang
(1891–1971)

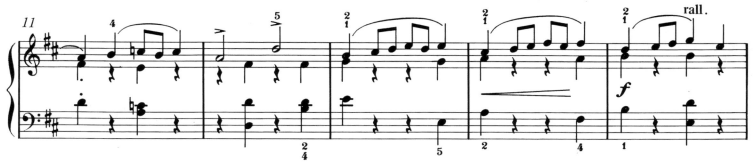

From Sketches for piano. Reproduced by permission of Novello and Company Limited.

1969
The Old Wheelbarrow

Hugh Seal
(1910–)

Astronauts Neil Armstrong and Edwin 'Buzz' Aldrin were the first men to set foot on the moon. They stayed on the lunar surface for 21½ hours.

Hugh Seal is a clergyman, and was a pupil of W. H. Reed—leader of the London Symphony Orchestra at the time Elgar was composing his masterpieces. Reed would often visit Elgar to play through new works, finding pieces of manuscript paper pasted all over the room.

Reproduced by permission of the composer.

A nocturne is a piece which suggests night-time, and is usually of a romantic and perhaps slightly mysterious character. The name was first used by the Irish composer John Field, and later by Chopin.

1990
Nocturne
Paul Harris
(1957–)

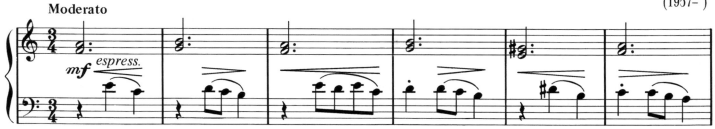

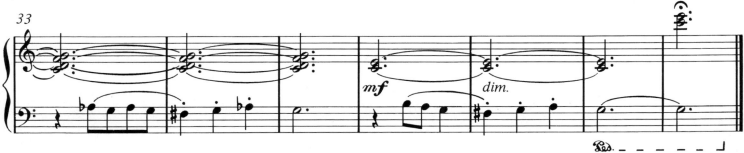

Reproduced and printed by
Halstan & Co. Ltd., Amersham, Bucks., England